Original title:
Bubbles of Memory

Copyright © 2025 Creative Arts Management OÜ
All rights reserved.

Author: Ophelia Ravenscroft
ISBN HARDBACK: 978-1-80587-462-1
ISBN PAPERBACK: 978-1-80587-932-9

Evaporating Thoughts

A sneeze blew away my prized balloon,
It danced in the air like a silly cartoon.
Chasing it down, I tripped on a cat,
Who sat there smirking, 'What do you think of that?'

My old notebook filled with doodles and dreams,
Now has coffee stains where it once had gleams.
I turned the page, it whispered a joke,
But then it yawned and went up in smoke!

Photos of friends with silly old hats,
Hide in my drawer next to some crafty spats.
We laugh and we giggle at all that we see,
While dodging the hairball from Fluffy the flea.

Chasing lost socks that waltz on the floor,
Their partners are gone, can't take it much more!
Each step is a giggle, a stumble, a trip,
While yearning for moments that fade with a flip.

Fleeting Echoes

Whispers of laughter, they float in the air,
Like socks in the dryer, a whimsical pair.
Each giggle a promise, a wink from the past,
A chase through the fields, too funny to last.

Silly old stories that twist and that bend,
A cat wearing glasses, we all must defend.
Yet shadows of moments spin round in delight,
For truth is a jester in dim candlelight.

Silken Threads of the Past

In patterns of laughter, we weave and we sway,
As time rolls away like a child at play.
Knots made of giggles and sprinkles of cheer,
With every bright tale, the sky seems more clear.

A shoe on a cat, a fish in the tree,
Format this nonsense in pure jubilee.
And as we reminisce, the chuckles return,
Like stickers on frosted cakes—oh, how they burn!

Ephemeral Glistens

Moments that twinkle, both silly and sweet,
Like candy on sidewalks, a fun little treat.
A dance in the rain while wearing one sock,
A snapshot of chaos on an old wooden rock.

Tickles of joy in the back of our minds,
Silly old faces, the quirkiest kinds.
Reminders that time is just one great big joke,
Wrapped in sweet memories, and laughter's the smoke.

A Float in the Past

Strange little moments that get in your head,
Like toast that keeps bouncing despite being fed.
A prance on a pogo, a slip on a shoe,
Each slip shows the magic of what we once knew.

Chasing the echoes of giggles we heard,
Like a butterfly laughs, not needing a word.
In the sea of our thoughts, where silliness swims,
We float on the waves while the world softly dims.

Encapsulated Reminiscence

In a jar, my thoughts collide,
Like fizzy drinks all inside.
I laugh at faces, strange and wide,
As time's sweet tricks have come to bide.

Forgetful socks and goldfish dreams,
Bouncing high on silly gleams.
The past is more than what it seems,
With giggles trapped in fizzy streams.

Moments Suspended in Time

Time once stole my favorite hat,
Now I see it worn by a cat.
Each tick-tock brings a quirky chat,
With memories curled, a joyful spat.

I find my bike in grandma's pond,
With turtles, laughter, silly prongs.
The world is full of silly songs,
Where nothing's right, but nothing's wrong.

The Fragile Dance of Recollection

A waltz of gaffes, oh what's this rue?
I tripped on tales, my shoes askew.
In twilight's glow, did we all stew?
With pratfalls crafted by the crew.

Hiccups echo, laughter spills,
As memory shakes and laughter thrills.
I juggle jokes, like tripping frills,
In dance of time, inflation kills.

Fleeting Fancies Adrift

Marshmallow dreams float on the breeze,
With giggles caught in playful trees.
Chasing memories as they tease,
While time just bumbles and never flees.

Chocolate stains on old school books,
Trampoline jumps and curious looks.
I read the past like silly crooks,
With each fond laugh, the future cooks.

The Weight of Wishful Thoughts

In my head, they float and sway,
Chasing giggles like a game of play.
Each silly thought, a tiny prize,
Wobbling high with painted skies.

With each wish, a wink and grin,
I trip on dreams, the fun begins.
A hop, a skip, and then a fall,
Who knew wishes could be tall?

They jostle, tease, and dance with glee,
Whispering secrets just for me.
Yet, when I catch them, poof!—they're gone,
As if they never were, just drawn.

Oh, the weight of thoughts that fly,
Like feathers plucked from clouds up high.
I laugh and sigh at what I bestow,
A circus act of thoughts in tow.

Iridescent Shadows in Silence

In quiet corners, they wink and gleam,
Shadows play tricks, weaving a dream.
A giggle here, a snicker there,
As silence hums a vibrant air.

They slip through moments, bright and sly,
Dancing through laughter, oh my, oh my!
When I look closer, they dart away,
Leaving behind a joke to play.

With colors that shimmer and twist so bold,
The giggly whispers turn stories old.
They tickle my heart, they ripple and sway,
Making the mundane a grand ballet.

And as they vanish, all in good fun,
I wish for more before they've run.
But in the silence, echoes remain,
Those iridescent sprites of joy and pain.

Fantasies in Suspension

Hanging like laundry on a line,
My thoughts dance like they're sipping wine.
Each one a tale, a jolly jest,
Swirling gently, at play like the rest.

The sky's the limit—unless it rains,
Then down they tumble, hurry, and strain!
With every drop, a laughter shared,
Marooned on rooftops, dreams impaired.

They tease my mind like little sprites,
Pirouetting through the starry nights.
Each twist and twirl, a merry game,
In the fog of dreams, they're never the same.

But once the sun shines clear and bright,
The fantasies scatter, taking flight.
Left behind only silly grins,
And echoes of joy where laughter spins.

Fleeting Images in a Dream

In realms where winks and nods collide,
Strange sights emerge and then subside.
A cat in boots, a fish that flies,
Tickled space where nonsense lies.

They flit like butterflies, quick and bright,
In the theater of slumber, a comical sight.
With candy clouds and soda streams,
Who knew that dreams could be such schemes?

But just as joy spills its beams,
They vanish like whispers, those silly dreams.
I reach for giggles, and they dissolve,
Leaving riddles that never solve.

Yet in my heart, their echoes stay,
A carnival dance in whimsical play.
Though fleeting, these images beam,
Forever sparkling in the seams.

Pools of Past Delight

In the garden of laughs, where giggles burst,
Old toys dance lightly, in laughter they thirst.
A wobbly chair takes a spin and then tips,
Chasing memories sweet like a kid's sugar trips.

Swings creak and sway, a symphony plays,
While sippy cups spill like the sun on some rays.
We reminisce loud, each chuckle a flare,
As we tumble through ages without a care.

Shimmering Hues of the Heart

Crayons and colors, an artist's delight,
With every sharp scribble, the world feels so right.
A unicorn dances on the walls of our time,
While jellybeans waltz to our favorite rhyme.

Each hue brings a giggle, a sparkle, a pop,
Grandma's old quilt makes our imagination drop.
We laugh till we ache, chasing dreams in the air,
As the world spins around in a vibrant affair.

Fleeting Shadows in the Breeze

The wind whispers secrets, through branches it sneaks,
Playing tricks on old faces, with whimsical peaks.
A shadowy figure, could it be a prank?
Or just my old buddy, stealing joy from the bank?

We chase after giggles; the sunlight shifts fast,
With cotton candy dreams, oh, how long will they last?
Giggles collide in the warm evening glow,
As we run through the dusk, where wild memories grow.

Chasing Elusive Echoes

In a game of tag with the past on a spree,
Laughter ricochets off the old maple tree.
A deer in the distance seems curious too,
With antics so silly, it joins in our crew.

We leap and we bound, as the echoes come clear,
Each trip and stumble brings forth a loud cheer.
Like butterflies flitting, we yearn to believe,
In the joy of our youth, as we dance and misleave.

Fragments of Light

In a teacup, time did dwell,
A toast to laughter, can you tell?
Marshmallow clouds and jelly beans,
Chasing giggles in silly scenes.

Frog on a skateboard zooms with glee,
Wobbling like it's time for tea,
Umbrellas sprout from paper straws,
Are you ready for applause?

Balloons wear hats, they twirl and sway,
They danced like fish on a breezy day,
Sing a tune to a dancing cat,
What a show, how about that?

Such memories wrapped in candy floss,
With every slip, we find our loss.
Giggles swirl in the afternoon,
Here's a wink and a cheerful tune.

Whispering Shadows

A shadow sneezes and shakes a tree,
With pumpkins laughing in jubilee,
Footprints scribble on the ground,
As echoes giggle all around.

Twirling hats on a scarecrow's head,
Dance of folly as the wind sped,
Bread rolls thrown at a passing car,
Guess that's what we call bizarre!

Socks mismatched, a fashion faux pas,
But who's to judge when you're a star?
Hopping around with a missing shoe,
Life's too funny; what can you do?

Butterflies play hide and seek,
Whispering secrets, oh so meek.
With every slip of time we find,
A chuckle left far behind.

Dance of the Unseen

Invisible critters in a silly race,
Tumble and twirl in a bright embrace,
A bee wearing shades, vibrant and bold,
Drinks fizzy nectar, oh, what a gold!

Starry socks on a dancing floor,
Twinkling toes say, "Let's dance more!"
With moons flying high and stars on fire,
Who knew that fun would inspire?

Jumping over puddles, splashing with flair,
The water giggles at the butterflies' stare,
Glancing up at a cotton-candy sky,
In this world, even clouds can fly!

Invisible tools make chaos divine,
Scattering laughs like glittery wine,
Time winks at us with playful delight,
As we frolic into the night.

Twinkling Serendipities

A squirrel in spectacles reads a map,
While jellybeans form a lovely trap,
Giggling daisies wiggle with flair,
Each one with secrets, none to share.

A sneaky breeze tickles the trees,
Dancing fibers float with ease,
Tickled by laughter, the sun looks down,
Wearing a smile instead of a frown.

Chickens juggle marshmallows high,
A ring of daisies, oh me, oh my!
With every chuckle that the world spins,
We're finding joy in the silliest wins.

Twinkling moments drift through the air,
Jokesters play in our hearts without a care,
So let the giggles catch up to me,
In this tapestry of glee.

Gossamer Threads of Nostalgia

In a jar kept on the shelf,
I caught a laugh or two.
A silly face made by myself,
With pigtails askew.

The cat wearing my mom's shoe,
Pranced across the floor.
A image that still feels new,
Like I've seen it before.

Sticky fingers and sweet delight,
Candy crumbs everywhere.
Running wild into the night,
Without a single care.

Old photos in the sun's embrace,
Fading like laughter's call.
Each snapshot a warm, fuzzy place,
Where I had the biggest ball.

Fragments Adrift in Air

A sock that skipped, a shoe that danced,
Frivolous tales to tell.
We twirled and leapt, it seemed by chance,
In our own silly spell.

The goldfish blinks, the doggy grins,
Plotting mischief galore.
With laughter and whispers, our fun begins,
Who could ask for more?

Lost marbles and crayons galore,
Painted walls scream our fun.
Adventurers on the hardwood floor,
From dusk till rising sun.

As leaves fell like confetti rain,
We jumped in piles so high.
Those fleeting giggles, pure, untamed,
I still hear as they fly.

Captured in a Breath

A sneeze that turned into a giggle,
Caught in a moment's sway.
We acted out our favorite riddle,
In a wild, humorous display.

Uninvited, a shoe flew by,
Landing atop a cat.
Gaps in stories, oh me, oh my!
How could we forget that?

With doughnuts stuck to noses,
And frosting on our ears,
Each mishap, like a flower, poses,
Blooming laughter through the years.

Madcap games that filled the air,
Whispers of joy run free.
From hide and seek, oh, what a pair!
A ruckus, you and me.

Liquid Memories Under the Surface

Plip-plop sound of laughter drawn,
From splashes in the pool.
Daredevil dives into the dawn,
Breaking all the rules.

Floating past a rubber duck,
Wobbly and bold.
The sun kissed all our luck,
Every memory retold.

With wild hair and gleeful squeals,
Chasing summer's delight.
Each splash a truth, a joke that heals,
What joy in simple sight.

As twilight paints the sky in hues,
We laugh without a care.
Those liquid gems, forever muse,
In splendor, bold and rare.

Shimmering Remnants

In the attic, dust takes flight,
Grandma's tales, a sheer delight.
Old shoes squeak on the grayed floor,
Musty laughter hides in the door.

A sock with stripes, too bright to wear,
Befriends a cat, with wild, frizzy hair.
Wobbly chairs tell secrets untold,
Every creak, a memory bold.

Forgotten cookie jars with smiles,
Chasing shadows down the aisles.
Lollipops in sunlit beams,
Tickling my most hilarious dreams.

A rubber duck with a goofy grin,
Floats in thoughts, let's dive in!
Friends from childhood, all returned,
Where up is down and laughs are earned.

Dreamscapes of Reflection

Floating through a jolly maze,
Wacky faces spin and gaze.
Lollipop rain falls from the sky,
Silly hats soar ever high.

A marshmallow cloud bursts with cheer,
Each giggle twirls, it's crystal clear.
Jellybeans dance in a funky groove,
As chuckles move, the days improve.

Fridge magnets with whispers sly,
Hold comic strips but why oh why?
Bananas do the cha-cha too,
In this realm where fun feels new.

Against the backdrop of silly sounds,
A rhyming sea of joy surrounds.
Chasing echoes with a grin,
In this land, the fun won't thin.

Effervescent Dreams

Soda pop and fizzy cheer,
Bouncin' here and bouncin' near.
Chattering whispers in the night,
Ticklish stars that sparkle bright.

An octopus with polka dots,
In my tea, it's swirling lots.
Dreams of dancing on a pie,
Floating high, oh me, oh my!

Noodle fights in cheese-filled skies,
Pasta planes that zoom and fly.
Cupcakes laugh, their sprinkles spry,
Wobble wobble, no "goodbye."

Toothbrush swords in this delight,
Fights of bubblegum take flight.
Every bite a tasty cheer,
In this world, there's nothing here!

Blurred Reflections

A mirror laughs with twisted glee,
Showcasing shapes too wild to see.
Mismatched socks in a wobbly line,
The world spins on, all quite fine.

Shopping carts with silly tunes,
Join the party under the moons.
Jumping jelly in a green parade,
Every song makes the moment cascade.

Whiskers tickle as cats prance by,
Chasing shadows that dance and fly.
Every flutter writes a rhyme,
In this giggle, lost in time.

Glancing glimpses of daffodils,
Time rewinds, old laughter thrills.
Here in the shuffle, life's a game,
Where whimsy and joy always reign.

Floating Reminders

In the air, a wobbly dance,
Chasing thoughts that boldly prance.
A hiccup here, a giggle there,
Joyful moments float in the air.

Splat! A memory tickles my ear,
Was it a joke or just a cheer?
The laughter bubbles, slips, and glows,
Where this one lands, nobody knows!

They shimmer, popping, bright as stars,
Recalling times of silly bars.
With every burst, a chuckle springs,
Who knew fun could come from such things?

So here we float, with smiles wide,
In a world where giggles glide.
Each reminder, a plucky surprise,
Crafting joy in disguise.

Ethereal Footprints

Tiny steps in a fluffy haze,
Leaving marks in a giggly maze.
Pitter-patter on the floor,
What was that? Oh! Just a roar!

Floating past, a ticklish tease,
Invisible paths swirling with ease.
Each footstep tells a quirky tale,
Of mischief and laughs that never fail.

A skip, a jump, a twist of fate,
Memory dances, it's never late.
In a world where silliness reigns,
We share the laughter, love, and gains.

Soft impressions, fleeting spree,
Bringing back the silly glee.
With every hop, the past will gleam,
As we sketch our joyful dream.

Reflections on the Surface

In a puddle, a sly grin waits,
Reflecting tales that always rate.
Wavy whispers in giddy streams,
Tickling our playful dreams.

With each ripple, a giggle grows,
What was that? A funny nose?
Dipping toes in a chuckly dance,
How surreal is this funny chance?

Mirrored moments in silly shades,
Revealing laughter that never fades.
Splashing memories in splendiferous ways,
As they brighten our drizzly days.

So let them shimmer, let them shine,
In puddle fun, we intertwine.
Every glance brings forth a grin,
With reflections, the joy begins.

Glistening Memories

They sparkle bright like candy rain,
Scoops of joy, who can complain?
Swirling colors, a shiny tease,
Bringing laughter with such ease.

Flickers of fun, like confetti flies,
A giggle heard, amidst the sighs.
A splash of charm from days gone past,
Each twirl of joy is meant to last.

Floating softly, a comical sight,
With every glimmer, it feels just right.
Twirling tales of jolly finesse,
Crafted moments, we must confess!

So let us dance in this sparkle spree,
Where every glint is pure esprit.
In the shine, our laughter gleams,
Creating a quilt of quirky dreams.

Fragments of Yesterday

In a jar of soggy socks,
I found my childhood rocks.
There's a rubber ducky too,
Wearing my old shoe.

Grandma's tales of flying pigs,
Dancing on unicycles, big.
I laughed till my sides turned blue,
What a wacky zoo!

Chasing ice cream trucks anew,
Till I tripped on a patch of goo.
Now my memories twist and twine,
Like my socks from laundry time.

Captured dreams in a cereal box,
With notes from my sock puppet talks.
Each giggle a twist, each giggle a spin,
What a silly world I'm in.

Luminous Thoughts

Bright balloons float above,
Each one a whisper of love.
The cat thinks it's his throne,
While I'm stuck with a cone.

Dancing on air with my lunch,
A sandwich began to munch.
While a pickle rolled away,
I laughed at its daring play.

In the toaster, my dreams burn,
Yet the crumbs have tales to churn.
Each bite a joke tossed high,
Like popcorn aiming for the sky.

Giggles echo in the stream,
Where jellybeans bounce and gleam.
With every silly spark in sight,
My thoughts take a joyful flight.

Moments in Suspension

Caught in a net of yarn,
With a cat that's causing harm.
Each tangle tells a tale,
Of adventures off the rail.

In the fridge, a debate rages,
Between old cheese and fresh pages.
The leftovers start to sing,
As the midnight snack bells ring.

I tried to juggle my keys,
But dropped them with comic ease.
Now they laugh beneath the couch,
With memories that they vouch.

Frozen smiles in the ice tray,
Giggling as they melt away.
Each moment holds a grin wide,
In the time of its mirthful ride.

Glimpses of the Past

A wig on the garden gnome,
That still dreams of a grand tome.
While flowers laugh in bright arrays,
And chase my blues away.

There's a bicycle with a bell,
That rings tales of a candy shell.
As I rode through sticky streets,
Dodging gum and funny treats.

Memories wrapped in candy floss,
With a wisdom that's quite glossed.
Each bite a chuckle in disguise,
With giggles hiding in their size.

Oh, the treasure chest of things,
Each memory fluttering, it sings.
In laughter we find the spark,
Leaving trails like a hippo in the park.

Transparent Reveries

In the attic, dust takes flight,
Old toys dance in faded light.
A rubber duck with a silly grin,
Makes me wonder where I've been.

A photo slips, it lands with a flop,
Grandma's hat, a colorful prop.
We giggle at the way she posed,
In polka dots—yes, she knows!

A record spins, the needle jumps,
Uncle Joe's dance? A series of thumps.
The cat joins in, with a lazy twirl,
No one warns her, she gives it a whirl.

And when the light fades, shadows creep,
Nostalgia tickles, and laughter leaps.
With each silly moment, a chuckle grows,
In this raucous dream where mischief flows.

The Air We Remember

Floating high on a summer's breeze,
A kite flops down, caught in the trees.
Squeals of joy, a paper plane,
Spinning round in the fog of brain.

Grandpa's stories, a fishing line,
Cast into moments, both silly and fine.
A grand mishap—a worm takes flight,
Caught a laugh at that comical sight.

At picnics, crumbs fly from the spreads,
Mom's hat gets whacked by her own kids' heads.
We giggle and snicker, it's all in good fun,
As ants march by, they consider a run.

The laughter bubbles, no one can stop,
Memories floating, they never drop.
With each silly tale and twist of fate,
We gather and chuckle, never too late.

Spheres of Softness

In the park, a soft ball bounces high,
Squeezed by laughter, it flies through the sky.
A puppy darts, it's his favorite game,
Chasing shadows without any shame.

A custard pie lands, splat on my face,
It's a sweet disaster, oh, what a chase!
We double over, rolling in mirth,
Who knew dessert could hold such worth?

In the backyard, bubbles drift away,
Each one a secret from yesterday.
I trip on a hose, and oh the sound!
My dance of awkwardness, tumbling down.

The night's filled with twinkling stars above,
We laugh till it hurts, this is our love.
In moments so light, we find our glow,
While bouncing softly, we steal the show.

Reverberations in Time

A ticking clock plays tricks on the mind,
With echoes of laughter, it's quite unconfined.
A dance in the kitchen, pots clanging loud,
Who knew cooking would gather a crowd?

A runaway sock, a plot so absurd,
Hiding beneath where no one has stirred.
We search and we laugh, what a silly plight,
Collecting these moments, pure joy takes flight.

The vacuum roars, a wild chase ensues,
While Dad makes a leap, forgetting his shoes.
In the evening glow, tales combo-size,
Each time it happens, we win in disguise.

In the folds of our lives, memories stick,
Woven with laughter, delightful and thick.
As echoes of time bring us back to play,
We cherish the fun in each quirky day.

Light as a Memory

A giggle drifts through time's embrace,
Like socks in a dryer, lost without grace.
Each laugh bounces, a wobbly friend,
Catching the sunlight, let's hope it won't end.

Confetti of thoughts, all in a dance,
Remembering moments, as if by chance.
A silly mishap, a pie to the face,
Echoes that linger, providing a trace.

The Sphere of What Was.

Round like a dream that just won't pop,
Filled with the laughter, the giggles don't stop.
When life served its jokes on a playful plate,
I found my good fortune—best served with fate.

A rubber chicken, a pratfall, a slip,
Moments that bubble, giving life a good grip.
Like candy-coated wishes from past candy shops,
We cherish the fun, as the laughter just hops.

Whispers in the Air

Tickles of joy float like feathers,
The secrets of laughter, in untethered weathers.
Silly stories shared, so light on the breeze,
Filling the room with invisible keys.

Chasing the echoes of times brightly spent,
A wink from the past, a moment's intent.
With each little giggle that dances around,
The stories of yore in the laughter are found.

Floating Echoes

Wobbly thoughts drifting on a whim,
Sailing through moments, where shadows are slim.
A jolly old joke, it swirls and it twirls,
In the whirlpool of laughter, as memory swirls.

Like soap bubbles popping with whimsy delight,
Each flicker of humor, a spark in the night.
In the circus of life, with smiles on parade,
The fun of today's joy is never delayed.

Chasing Wisps

In the backyard, a chase begins,
With cotton candy dreams on the winds.
Laughter spills from our goofy little crew,
While we tumble and trip, oh what a view!

The dog thinks we're hiding a treat somewhere,
But it's just silly games, floating in air.
We chase the shadows that make us squeal,
As laughter fills spaces that we can feel.

We leap over puddles, we dodge the sun,
Falling like ducks to a splashy fun run.
When the ice cream drips down to our toes,
We giggle and dance, it's a grandiose show!

In a world full of whims, we lose track of time,
Caught in the folly, a bright summer rhyme.
Every twist and turn brings more delight,
As we chase our wisps into the night.

Fleeting Glimmers

A tickle of sparkles in the air we see,
Floating like fireflies, wild and free.
We hold the moment before it's lost,
In a whirlwind of giggles, we pay no cost.

Tiny adventures in a candy land,
Where marshmallows grow and life is grand.
We weave stories with sugar on our lips,
Imagine ourselves as witty little quips.

Every glance turns to laughter, a mirror's jest,
While silly faces put our patience to test.
A dance with shadows, we twirl and glide,
Chasing glimmers with friends right by our side.

Each moment we catch feels like a prank,
With wishes and winks, we're climbing the rank.
In a whirlwind of glee, we spark and shimmer,
With fleeting glimmers, our hearts start to glimmer!

Soft Light in the Dark

When the day bids adieu, shadows grow tall,
We gather together, in the hush of it all.
With whispers and tales, a blanket of fun,
The night wraps around, like a soft, cozy bun.

Fireflies twinkle like secrets we share,
We giggle in darkness, a silly affair.
Robins may sulk, but we dance in delight,
With shadows to guide us, our spirits take flight.

Every random joke lingers, light as a breeze,
Underneath starlit skies, our hearts feel at ease.
A sprinkle of mischief in moonbeams so soft,
In laughter, we float, like balloons aloft.

In this pocket of night, all worries dissolve,
We weave threads of joy, a puzzle to solve.
With each soft light shining, we shine even brighter,
In the dark, we find laughter, our dreams take flight, sir!

The Weight of Air

There's a weight to the air when we jump and we play,
Like gravity's laughing, keeping dreams at bay.
We bounce like rubber, defying all rules,
Transforming our lives into whimsical schools.

A gust of wind whispers jokes in our ear,
As we tumble and roll, casting off doubt and fear.
We hold our breath, hearts fluttering high,
Like balloons in the sky, oh, how we fly!

We test our luck on an inflatable sea,
Where reality slips like a giggle from me.
We thick-skinned tumble with grace and a shout,
As laughter erupts, there's no shadow of doubt.

So we frolic along, through whimsical air,
With joy in our hearts, it's a fun, funny affair.
Each leap and each bound, a memory made,
In the weight of the air, as we dance and parade!

Dreams Encased in Glass

In the attic, a jar with a twist,
Holds giggles and hiccups, a long-lost mist.
I reached for a snack, but found a deep sigh,
My sandwich of laughter just floated on by.

A cat wearing socks danced on the floor,
While elephants tiptoed right out through the door.
Each snack of absurdity, pure delight,
I laughed till I teared up, what a strange sight!

Oh, shiny reflections, where thoughts twirl and spin,
A pickle in glasses made all the fun begin.
The whispers of childhood wrapped tight in a jar,
Ticket to silliness, just hop in the car!

So keep your spirits and wild dreams alive,
Like peanut butter jellybeans, we will thrive.
Unlock every chuckle, don't let it drift,
For giggles encased are the silliest gift.

Echoes in a Floating Sphere

In a sphere made of laughter, my thoughts start to glide,
With tickles and snorts we tumble and slide.
A rubber duck symphony sings through the air,
As we dance on the clouds in our fuzzy despair.

Jellybeans bouncing, a carnival scene,
A trampoline jump that feels oh-so-keen.
With banana peels slipping beneath our feet,
We whirl in the echo of laughter so sweet.

Toots and snickers, the soundtrack we play,
In a bubble of joy, we just float and sway.
Each giggle a wave, each laugh a new spark,
We'll sail through the skies till the daylight goes dark.

Lost in the shimmer of jokes that we share,
It's a party of silliness, come join if you dare.
A world filled with whimsy, oh what a delight,
In this sphere of our minds, we take silly flight!

Whispers of the Lost Moment

Here in a pocket, the whispers reside,
Of marshmallow creatures that bounce and collide.
A wink from the past, like a juggler's trick,
Where time flies on pogo sticks, quick and sick.

An old sock puppet sings songs of the day,
Mixed-up mischief in a comical way.
Time swirls like noodles in a wacky pot,
With memories bubbling, I check for the lot.

The spoonful of laughter gets lost in the stew,
As jellybeans march in a line, just for you.
The echoes of giggles slide down like a slide,
In a blink, they vanish, like mushrooms, they hide.

So capture the moments, the quirky, the sweet,
For life's a wild circus of chocolate and beat.
With shadows of humor that flit with delight,
Let's hold on to these whispers until the last light.

Iridescent Reflections

In a dream that's like candy, sweet shades all around,
Laughter glitters and sparkles, where silliness is found.
With hiccups like fountains that bubble and burst,
We dance on the floor, for humor is a must!

Mirrors of mischief, where giggles collide,
A carnival of colors, a whimsical ride.
With jelly-filled wishes and sweet, silly schemes,
We float through the madness, like rainbows of dreams.

Bright voices of echoes, like chimes in the breeze,
Where memories ripple and worm their way, tease.
The tickle of laughter, a giggle parade,
Reflecting the joy that we've lovingly made.

So let's splash in the puddles, all grins and no frowns,
In our bright world of color, let's dance, twirl and clown.
For in these reflections, where nonsense is king,
We'll dive into whimsy and let our hearts sing!

Gossamer Chains

In the attic, old hats dance,
Twirling to a forgotten trance.
A shoe from modernity's past,
Laughs at the memories amassed.

Grandpa's socks, a riotous sight,
With stripes that could cause a fright.
They wiggle and kick on their own,
Recalling the mischief they've sown.

Spoons sing tunes from a bygone meal,
With flavors only nostalgia can feel.
Each clang a chuckle, each clang a grin,
Echoing laughter wrapped tightly within.

A curtain flutters, whispers a joke,
A gobble of giggles, stirs in the smoke.
Together they chuckle, this whimsical crew,
Their antics replay every time they brew.

A Flicker of Yesterdays

A photo flips, the laughter bursts,
Funny faces, quirkily immersed.
A chicken dance in Sunday best,
They twirl and prance, what a jest!

That old record spins, starts to hop,
The crazy rhythms make us stop.
Grandma's wiggle, a sight to behold,
In a moment, her youth retold.

A tinfoil hat plays peek-a-boo,
Crowning a head that's far from blue.
Memories swirl, with sparkles and mirth,
In this playground of whimsical earth.

A rubber chicken joins the show,
Telling tales only we know.
Each giggle, a flash; each laugh, a spark,
Lighting up the corners of dark.

Glistening Moments

With marshmallow fluff stuck in hair,
We burst into giggles, life without care.
Sticky fingers, sweets galore,
Every bite opens a memory door.

A rubber band king on the throne,
With paper crowns made from things we've grown.
Drawing laughter from silly schemes,
Each conversation, full of dreams.

Soda geysers, pop and spray,
Frothing laughter carried away.
In playful chaos, truth we find,
Wondrous joys fill heart and mind.

Glittery confetti from the past,
Raining down, precious and vast.
With each little piece, a story to tell,
Of laughter, of sparkle, of time spent well.

Shapes of the Mundane

The toaster giggles, toast pops high,
Jam drips down as mornings fly.
A spatula flips with glee and grace,
In the kitchen, laughter finds its place.

Socks go missing, on a wild spree,
They form a club, just wait and see.
Each lone one laughs at a partner's fate,
In the drawer of lost, they celebrate.

A whisk winks and a blender grins,
Stirring up mischief as it spins.
Surprises leap from the cupboard doors,
And echoes of joy ring on the floors.

The mundane hums a joyous tune,
In every corner, a sprinkle of moon.
Where laughter blooms from the simple things,
And the heart of humor gently sings.

A Weightless Tapestry

In a realm of laughter and jest,
Hopes float like balloons, the best.
Each giggle, a stitch in the air,
A fabric of joy, light and rare.

Jellybeans dance, their colors bright,
A tapestry woven with sheer delight.
Silly faces make us all grin,
As we thread through the stars, let's begin.

Like kites soaring high, we play,
With dreams spun in the sun's warm ray.
Chasing shadows and whispers of cheer,
Life's whimsy creates memories here.

With a twirl and a skip, we embrace,
The art of remembrance, a playful grace.
As laughter echoes through the mist,
In this light-hearted world, we persist.

Emotions on the Edge of Bursting

A giggle escapes, so light and bright,
Emotions are bubbles, oh what a sight!
Laughter hides in corners, waiting to pop,
While we dance on the edge, never stop.

Tickles surprise us like confetti in air,
Happiness bounces, no room for despair.
With each little laugh, joy takes its flight,
Turns the mundane into sheer delight.

The silly faces that friends like to make,
Remind us of joy, for fun's own sake.
As sparkles explode, let's cherish this day,
Emotions like bubbles, come out to play.

So join in the dance, let the fun unfurl,
In this joyous circus, let memories swirl.
With each fleeting moment, we let them blend,
Each laugh a reminder, each giggle's a friend.

Transparent Treasures

Hidden gems in the corners of mind,
Transparent treasures, joy intertwined.
With each little chuckle, remember the past,
Moments like candy, sweet and steadfast.

A quirky story, a heart-shaped grin,
Each laugh is a treasure, let the fun begin.
Whirling through memories, light as a breeze,
In this treasure chest, we find our ease.

Floating along like a whimsical tune,
Life's joys pop like balloons in June.
The silly slips of time, we gather near,
Transparent treasures, we hold so dear.

With a wink and a nudge, we dance in delight,
These memories glitter, radiant and bright.
In the canvas of laughter, let's paint the sky,
For in this collection, our hearts learn to fly.

The Glassy Veil of Remembrance

Through a glassy veil, we peer in with glee,
The echoes of laughter, wild and free.
Each moment a ripple in time's flowing stream,
Reflecting the oddest, yet sweetest dream.

Silly shenanigans bubble up high,
With quirks and antics that never say die.
The veil of remembrance, it flutters and spins,
Capturing essence of all our whims.

A tickle-filled reminder of all that we share,
In the whirlwind of laughter, we've none to spare.
The moments so fleeting, they slip right away,
But through the glassy veil, they forever stay.

Lift your spirits up, let your heart be light,
In this whimsical dance, we shine ever bright.
For in these sweet memories that glimmer and flow,
We find joy in the laughter, the love that we sow.

Delicate Traces

In the kitchen, a spoon takes flight,
Bouncing off waffles, oh what a sight!
Maple syrup glistens like gold,
With each giggle, a story unfolds.

Grandpa's mustache, a snappy twirl,
Tickling the cat, oh what a whirl!
We dash through the halls, a playful race,
Chasing shadows with laughter and grace.

Lost in the attic, a box of old toys,
Raggedy dolls and forgotten joys.
A slinky that dances, a yo-yo that spins,
Reviving our youth and the mischief within.

Under the sun, we romp without care,
Silly remarks float in warm summer air.
These fleeting moments, like whispers of rhyme,
Carried away on the winds of our time.

Ephemeral Worlds

A paper boat sails on a puddle so grand,
With a plastic fish taking its stand.
The rain starts to giggle, it tickles my nose,
Like a cheeky secret that nobody knows.

In the park, there's a swing that won't sway,
While squirrels debate if it's time to play.
A slide that squeaks jokes from its rusty past,
Echoes of laughter that forever last.

Marbles once precious now gather dust,
Days filled with frolic, forget we must.
Each turn of a card brings a flash of delight,
In a game of wait, making wrong into right.

With ice cream cones melting, we laugh till we cry,
As sticky hands reach for the brightening sky.
Just like the flavors that dance on our tongue,
These sweet little moments make us feel young.

Vapor Trails of Time

A kite takes off with a wobble and dip,
As a cloud laughs hard at its awkward flip.
Colorful trails in the azure above,
Like quicksilver giggles of things that we love.

Chasing each other through fields of tall grass,
Jumping in puddles, like children, we pass.
The sun plays hide and seek with our faces,
As we collect tales from funny old places.

Whispers of donuts and hot dogs galore,
We march through the streets, our feet feeling sore.
With every step, bright memories are made,
In a carnival dance, our worries all fade.

Laughter is sticky like gum on a shoe,
Leaving its mark in the craziest hue.
A snapshot of joy, trapped in our minds,
A treasure of times that no one can find.

Fleeting Imprints

On the fridge, a masterpiece, crayons in hand,
Cats in a parade, oh, isn't it grand?
With googly eyes staring from paper so torn,
Each scribble a journey, where laughter is born.

Grandma's old slippers, too big for my feet,
Make excellent vehicles for a racing cheat.
Through archways of giggles, we scatter like seeds,
Planting our joy in the wild flowering weeds.

A game of charades with dad's funny hat,
He dances with flair, oh where is he at?
The records spin stories of nights long gone by,
With melodies sweet, they enchant and they fly.

Under the stars, with our voices all high,
We topple like towers, and we giggle and sigh.
These fleeting imprints will sparkle like dew,
A funny mosaic of moments so true.

Ethereal Fragments

In a jar of dreams, I find my socks,
Dancing with laughter, like cheeky fox.
They giggle and twirl, a sight to behold,
Whispers of secrets, that never grow old.

A toast to the past, with a fizzy stew,
Frothy and sweet, like a morning dew.
I sip on the giggles, they tickle my nose,
Childlike delight, in these fragments that pose.

Old photographs wave like a playful breeze,
At family gatherings, they bring me to knees.
Remember the times when grandma's hat flew,
Chasing it down, oh what ruckus it drew!

With each funny moment, I gather and cling,
Mismatched socks, and the songs that we sing.
These ethereal oddities light up the gray,
Turning the mundane to a bright cabaret!

Small Wonders

A rubber duck floats in a tub of dreams,
With a quack and a splash, it bursts at the seams.
Bath time ballet with bubbles galore,
While dad sings off-key, we laugh 'til we roar.

In pockets of wonder, I find silly notes,
Doodles and riddles, worn-out old coats.
Each scribbled giggle is a treasure to keep,
Tickling my thoughts like a cat, it creeps.

Crayons on paper, a masterpiece bold,
A unicorn dancing, or so I am told.
Yet somehow, it looks like my old dog, Ted,
Wearing a tutu, and a crown on his head!

Whimsical tales wrapped in candy-bright cheer,
Snippets of laughter that I hold so dear.
These small wonders remind me with glee,
That life's fleeting moments are silly and free!

Flowing Memories

A river of giggles flows through my mind,
Each ripple a story, uniquely designed.
Water fights in summer, we splash and we play,
As ducks quack their laughter, they join in the fray.

Old bicycles wobble down streets painted gold,
With rusted-up baskets, and stories retold.
I ride with my friends, in a crooked line,
Each squeaky wheel echoes, 'This moment is mine!'

Puddles of laughter catch raindrops that fall,
Jumping right in, oh, the splashes enthrall!
While clouds whisper secrets of silly delights,
We dance on the sidewalks, through magical nights.

Memories flowing, like juice from a peach,
The sweetness of laughter is just out of reach.
Yet I chase every giggle, and hold them so dear,
These flowing recollections bring joy year to year!

Shattered Glass Prisms

With shards of delight, I reflect on the past,
Each glimmer a laugh, like balloons flying fast.
Dad trips on his laces, we shout and we cheer,
As rainbows of joy shimmer bright and unclear.

The cat skitters by, on a mission so grand,
Chasing the light with a paw deftly planned.
She leaps through reflections, a furry little star,
In a house full of giggles, it's never too far.

Mom's tales of mishaps, like soup on the wall,
Spaghetti monsters making silly us fall.
Each clumsy attempt, caught in vibrant display,
A prism of memory that colors the day.

So here's to the moments that flash and that glide,
Through laughter and tears, let our hearts feel the tide.
In shattered glass prisms, our stories entwine,
Like silly old jokes that simply age fine!

Translucent Dreams

In the backyard, glee takes flight,
Chasing orbs that shimmer bright.
Laughter echoes, a playful streak,
Floating whims, hide and seek.

Each a story, a giggle shared,
Fleeting thoughts, no one impaired.
They dance and swirl, make mischief new,
Like cotton candy skies, so sweet and blue.

With a tap, they burst, oh what a sight!
Setting free memories, pure delight.
A wish on each, as colors bend,
Catching smiles, they never end.

So gather round, let joy unfold,
In transparent dreams, let laughter be bold.
For in each pop, there's always the hint,
Of moments that shimmer with every glint.

Light as a Whisper

Dancing softly in the sun,
Whispers of joy, oh what fun!
Floating lightly, but what a tease,
Roaming free on the summer breeze.

Tickling noses, a playful prank,
Mischievous giggles at the bank.
Eyes wide open, a gleeful glance,
As they glide like a comical dance.

They pop like secrets, giggles burst,
Memories waiting to quench our thirst.
With every splash, a laugh explodes,
In this world of charm that freely strodes.

So grab a handful, don't be shy,
Crafting silliness as they fly high.
For what is life, if not this play?
A gentle nudge, the heart's ballet.

Ink on Water

In a world so wobbly and wet,
Silly quirks, you can't forget!
Marking laughter, a splashy spree,
Painting joys on a spirited sea.

Each little drop, a comic twist,
Like a clown fish, you can't resist.
Words like ink on a page of blue,
They wiggle and wobble, just like you.

With a splat and a giggle, they divide,
In circles of fun, our hearts collide.
Scribbled memories, so light and spry,
A joyful mess beneath the sky.

So let them swirl, let them spin,
In this playful world, we all win.
For laughter flows like the ink in a quill,
Creating moments that time cannot kill.

Celestial Echoes

Stars above with a wink and shout,
Silly cosmos, twirling about.
Planets giggle, swirling in cheer,
As comets zip by, no fear near.

Each little twinkle, a laugh so bright,
In the night sky, with pure delight.
Echoes of joy from distant lands,
As stardust dances on our hands.

A meteor's tail, a playful tease,
Swooping down like a summer breeze.
Round and round with cosmic flair,
In the silence, we find the rare.

So let's shoot for dreams, wild and free,
In this universe, just you and me.
With echoes of laughter, we trace our fate,
Writing our stories, never too late.

Spirals of Nostalgia

In a jar, the past does dance,
Marbles rolling with a glance.
Old shoes squeak, a rubber pie,
Chasing giggles, oh so spry.

Silly hats on heads held high,
Jumping puddles, watch them fly!
Napping cats with dreams so sweet,
Chasing tails that skip a beat.

Each crackle brings a laugh anew,
Like echoes of a peekaboo.
Memories prance in awkward glee,
As time whirls on, so carefree.

Old photographs in funny frames,
Wearing hats with silly names.
Tickle fights and painted walls,
Sounding out those distant calls.

Laughter in the Mist

A foggy morn, the drizzles tease,
Umbrella battles in the breeze.
Puddles giggle, splashes fly,
As rainy days make memories sigh.

Slippery socks on wooden floors,
Echoes of our playful roars.
Finding joy in every slip,
An accidental cartwheel trip.

Lemonade spills on sunny cheeks,
Cucumber sandwiches, giggling freaks.
Chasing rainbows in a sigh,
Wishing clouds would join the high.

When laughter lingers in the air,
We dance in mist without a care.
Whimsical thoughts on the breeze ride,
As we cherish, side by side.

Transient Treasures

A shoebox under the old bed,
Filled with trinkets and some dread.
Silly notes stuck in the seams,
Whispering long-forgotten dreams.

Plastic toys with broken feet,
Each one a story, oh so sweet.
Lollipop wrappers, candies past,
Moments captured, too quick to last.

Socks that vanished, where did they go?
Under the couch, hiding, oh no!
Another laugh at a silly fate,
Trying to remember, we just wait.

With each treasure, giggles wake,
Nostalgic savors, make no mistake.
In the game of loss and find,
We laugh at life, so intertwined.

Celestial Whispers

Stars above and dreams so wide,
Matching socks we try to hide.
Cosmic hiccups, giggles too,
Astronauts in pajamas cue.

Moonlit dance on kitchen tiles,
Silly spins and toothy smiles.
Dreamy brews of chocolate joy,
Imagination, a wondrous toy.

Whirling thoughts in night's embrace,
Finding laughter in empty space.
Comets trace a path of fun,
As we bask in laughter, spun.

Whispers float from glimmering skies,
Echoing joy, no need for ties.
In the chuckle of the light,
We find our spark, so pure, so bright.

Echoes of a Faded Past

In the attic, old shoes lay,
Squeaking tales of youth and play.
A sock puppet with a grin,
Claims he's where all fun begins.

Dusty dance moves in the air,
Grandpa's wig, beyond compare.
Laughter drips like melting ice,
Every slip, oh, such a slice!

Remember when we both fell down,
While pretending to be clowns?
The mirror cracked from all the glee,
Did we really trip, or was it me?

So here we sit, all laughs and sighs,
Harnessing our inner spies.
With every giggle, tales unfold,
From those days, forever bold.

Illusionary Trails

Yesterday's coffee was quite the thrill,
Sipped it slowly, then spilled with skill.
The cat jumped high, in a surprise,
As if it saw the world's demise.

My cereal danced upon the shelf,
Thought it'd talk, it just knew itself.
Each spoonful whispered, something odd,
"Do you believe? Come on, be bod!"

Pancakes flipped to reach the sky,
While syrup rivers just slipped by.
The fork had dreams of being a spoon,
Planning parties with a silver moon.

In this world of funny sights,
Where breakfast believes it has rights.
I'll pour my joy into a bowl,
And dance with mirth, that's my goal.

Soft Sighs of Yesterday

Old toys are relics, what a mess,
Giraffes stuck in a playful dress.
The rubber duck quacks, a brilliant song,
While the action figures pretend they belong.

Marbles whisper secrets galore,
One confessed it rolled out the door.
The yo-yo spins, trying hard to impress,
Though tangled up, it still finds success.

An old clock ticks, counting the fun,
Tick-tock, tick-tock, races begun.
With every glance at a faded toy,
I find the giggles, the endless joy.

So here I sit, surrounded by stash,
With a sippy cup and a splash.
Life's a patch of laughter, it's true,
And I am just teasing you.

The Essence of Now

Today I woke up on the wrong side,
With mismatched socks and a lopsided guide.
The toast jumped, trying to escape,
Wondered if it looked good in a cape.

The mirror laughed when I said cheese,
Told me to dress down, if you please.
The clock is late, or am I just fast?
Guess I wear chaos like it's cast.

A plant decides to sprout a joke,
Every time I step close, it spoke.
With every sip of my lemon tea,
Laughter spills—oh, let it be free!

So here I sit, in splendid now,
With quirks and quirks, take a bow.
Today's a show, a silly spree,
Join the laughter, come dance with me!

The Lightness of Being

In a teacup, big dreams swirl,
Laughter dances, time does a twirl.
Sweet confections, oh so light,
Tiny moments take to flight.

Rolling down a hill of cream,
Chasing shadows, it's a dream.
Wiggly smiles, giggles abound,
Joy is found all around.

Fluffing feathers in the air,
A sneeze turns into a scare.
Chasing echoes, silly schemes,
Life is woven with our themes.

In each twinkling star we find,
A giggle caught, a twist of mind.
With a wink and playful cheer,
The lightness lives, forever near.

Cascading Memories

Down the stream of silly thoughts,
Catch a fish with flashy spots.
Tangled tales in muddy shoes,
Laughter flows, we cannot lose.

Butterflies wearing tiny hats,
Chasing ants and playful cats.
Wading through a sea of socks,
Life's a carnival, full of rocks.

Jumping puddles, splashing fun,
Underneath the shining sun.
Tickled by a gentle breeze,
Memories swirl with playful tease.

In the garden, gnomes do sway,
Whispers of a brighter day.
In this dance of joy and cheer,
Cascading laughs, we hold dear.

Illusions of the Heart

A wobbly jelly on the floor,
Bouncing dreams behind the door.
Silly love notes drifting by,
With a grin and a sigh.

Hopscotch games on clouded paths,
Tickle fights and silly baths.
When the moon starts to giggle,
Rainbows swirl and make us wiggle.

With a wink, we spin around,
Hearts afloat, we're unbound.
Juggling thoughts like flying pies,
We wear laughter in our eyes.

In this theater of our mind,
All the joy we seek, we find.
Through the frolic and the art,
We dance with illusions of the heart.

Moments in the Breeze

Dandelions float like wishes,
Whispers of invisible fishes.
Crickets chirp a merry tune,
Beneath the light of a playful moon.

Frogs in hats and socks askew,
Join the dance in morning dew.
With each gust, a chance to play,
Moments waltz and drift away.

Sailing kites with colors bright,
Sipping tea in pure delight.
Caught in laughter, we all freeze,
Cherished times, they flow with ease.

As the sun begins to set,
We recall the fun, no regret.
In this breeze, we let it tease,
Moments linger with such ease.

Shattered Timepieces

Clocks are spinning, time's in a whirl,
Tick-tock giggles in a dizzying swirl.
Moments like candy, sticky and sweet,
Falling apart at the lightest of feet.

Yet every tick sounds like muffled cheer,
Echoes of laughter that seem to appear.
Timepieces shattered, their hands in a race,
Chasing the joy that we can't quite trace.

With every chime, a mischief's unleashed,
The past is a banquet, we never quite feast.
Cracking wide smiles at the silliest things,
Grinning at life's most ridiculous flings.

So let's toast to clocks lost in their fight,
Dancing and twirling into the night.
In this comical chaos, we find our delight,
Laughter is timeless, a pure, joyful sight.

Spheres of Forgotten Laughter

Round as a marble, a giggle takes flight,
Bouncing off walls in a fit of delight.
Memories float on a sea of pure glee,
Whirling and twirling, just you and me.

Each laugh is a bubble that pops in the air,
Tickling our senses, a moment laid bare.
Spheres of the past, in colors so bright,
Bouncing through time, a comical sight.

In our silly chase, oh what a parade,
Childhood's confetti, in laughter displayed.
Every little chuckle, a treasure to keep,
Rolling down hills where the antics run deep.

So here's to the laughter that dances and spins,
Chasing those echoes, where memory begins.
In this playful world, we twirl with delight,
Spheres of our laughter, shining so bright.

The Weight of Fleeting Joy

Joy sits heavy, yet floats like a kite,
Tugging at heartstrings with all of its might.
Lifting our spirits, oh what a tease,
Heavy with laughter, like wind in the trees.

Moments pass quickly, they dash and they dive,
The weight of each giggle helps us to thrive.
Chasing the fun, with wild, reckless cheer,
Wobbling through time like a clown at the fair.

Yet in the balance, we sway to the tune,
Of jest and of joy, beneath the bright moon.
Fleeting delight, in circus-like flair,
Tickles and chuckles, entwined in midair.

Oh, the weight of these whims that we juggle with glee,
Laughter's the anchor, it sets our hearts free.
So let the world spin with its merry refrain,
In this delightful dance, we rise up again.

Soft Echoes of Yesteryears

Whispers of laughter weave through the haze,
Soft echoes flutter in whimsical plays.
Each giggle a note from a past serenade,
Filling the room with the games that we've made.

Tickled by memories, light as a breeze,
Jokes from long ago put our minds at ease.
Echoes of silliness, drifting like dreams,
Painting our thoughts in kaleidoscope themes.

With every recollection, a smile will bloom,
Around funny corners, we chase through the room.
Past shenanigans dance in our heads,
Sowing sweet laughter where nostalgia spreads.

So let's gather 'round for this light-hearted jest,
In soft echoes' embrace, we feel truly blessed.
Cracking up softly, like petals unfurled,
In the garden of smiles, let's brighten the world.

Echoes of a Timeless Dance

In a whirl of socks and shoes,
A tango with my cereal fuse,
I twirled with a spoon, struck a pose,
As milk splashed up, my heart arose.

A waltz with shadows in the fridge,
Where leftover pizza danced on the edge,
It slid away with a giggling grin,
Crying, 'Don't let your diet win!'

Now I twirl with dust bunnies bold,
In my slippers, feeling so old,
They whispered secrets of days gone by,
While I laughed and let out a sigh.

So here's to all that we've misplaced,
The lost socks and crumbs we've chased,
Every slip and every slide,
A joyful dance we can't abide.

Softly Bursting Thoughts

A sneeze of ideas makes them pop,
Like popcorn kernels on the hop,
They leap and dance, a charming spree,
While I giggle at my own glee.

A thought rolled round like jelly beans,
It bounced away, cracking my seams,
Caught one mid-air, it flopped and rolled,
Telling tales from days of old.

Chasing dreams on a silly kite,
They twirled and twinkled in the night,
Each spiraled laugh a sweet delight,
As thoughts took flight, oh what a sight!

Grab your hat, hold on tight,
For thoughts may burst and take their flight,
Embrace the whimsy, let it show,
Our minds are sweet, like ice cream flow.

Crystal Clear Recollections

In a frame of glass where giggles gleam,
I caught a glimpse of an old daydream,
Marshmallow clouds and a rainbow's bend,
With every laugh, the edges blend.

I spotted a hat that once made me fly,
It whisked me past clouds, oh me, oh my!
With candy-coated wishes, I soared so high,
But gravity laughed, and I said goodbye.

A jar of smiles collected with care,
Each flicker of joy, a spark in the air,
I danced with memories, silly and bright,
In the glow of laughter, pure delight.

So here's to the treasures, the quirky and bold,
The tales of mischief that never grow old,
For in the glass, reflections revive,
A crystal clear glimpse of being alive.

Spheres of Light

In the corner, a glow that feels just right,
A gathering of moments, spheres of light,
They bob and weave like a playful dream,
Painting my world with a laughter theme.

Each glimmer tells a joke, a friendly tease,
Of rubber chickens and sneezing bees,
They spin around, a radiant ball,
Laughing as I trip, oh do I fall!

With every twinkle, a wink in disguise,
Chasing the sun, we laugh at the skies,
These little orbs of forgotten cheer,
Whispering secrets, 'Don't take life here!'

So I bounce with them, in a joyous flight,
These spheres of wonder that ignite delight,
For in each laugh, we find our bliss,
In the dance of memories, we swing and kiss.

www.ingramcontent.com/pod-product-compliance
Lightning Source LLC
Chambersburg PA
CBHW070308120526
44590CB00017B/2593